THE BIG DINOSAUR BOOK

By Susanne
Santoro Whayne

Illustrated by
James Spence

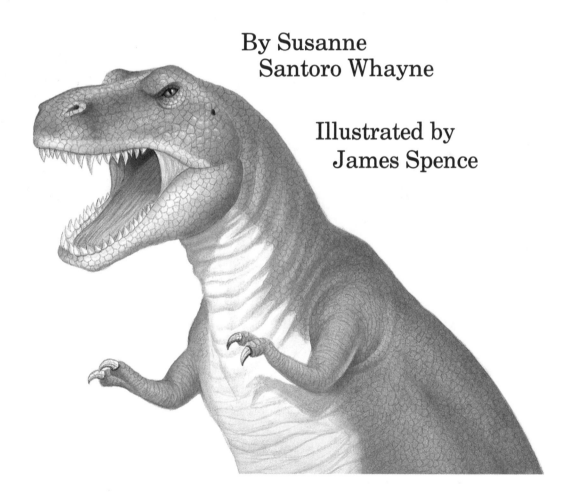

Text copyright © 1995 by Susanne Santoro Whayne. Illustrations copyright © 1995 by James Spence.
Published by Troll Associates, Inc. WhistleStop is a trademark of Troll Associates. All rights reserved.
Printed in the United States of America.   10 9 8 7 6 5 4 3 2 1

A Nutshell Book

Metric Conversion
1 inch = 25.4 mm
1 foot = 30.5 cm
1 mile = 1.61 km
1 ton = .91 metric ton

Herrerasaurus

A very long time ago, a dinosaur named Herrerasaurus (her-rare-rah-SAWR-us) lived in a forest of evergreens and tall ferns. Herrerasaurus was a hunter that could run fast on its strong back legs.

Herrerasaurus has been gone from Earth for 230 million years. How do we know about an animal that lived so long ago? No one has ever seen a live dinosaur, but we can learn about them by studying their fossils.

After Herrerasaurus died, layers of mud and sand covered its bones. Over millions of years the bones hardened and turned to rock. In 1986 scientists removed the fossil bones and examined them. The bones told scientists what Herrerasaurus might have looked like and how it lived.

Maiasaura

Once scientists thought that dinosaur parents were like turtles. They would have laid their eggs and left the hatchlings to fend for themselves. Now scientists think that some dinosaurs stayed with their eggs and cared for their young.

Maiasaura (mah-ee-uh-SAWR-uh) laid her eggs in a nest, then carefully covered them up with leaves and plants. The mother may have guarded the nest, and when the young ones hatched, she fed and protected them.

Apatosaurus

When it was time to move, some dinosaurs such as
Apatosaurus (ah-PAT-uh-sawr-us) traveled in large herds.
They kept their young in the center of the herd, where they
were safe from enemies, just as elephants do today.

Many plant-eating dinosaurs spent their days grazing peacefully. Stegosaurus (STEG-uh-sawr-us) walked with its head low, slowly nibbling plants. If threatened, this dinosaur could strike a powerful blow with its spiked tail.

Stegosaurus

Diplodocus (dih-PLOD-oh-kus) was a gigantic creature, ninety feet long. If there had been a baseball field for Diplodocus to nap on, it could have laid its head on home plate and touched first base with its tail!

Diplodocus

Even though Diplodocus was huge, it was hunted by
hungry meat-eating dinosaurs. For safety, Diplodocus
traveled in herds. Diplodocus could also stretch its long neck
over the treetops to watch for enemies such as Deinonychus.

Iguanodon

Deinonychus (dyne-ON-ik-us) was one of the deadliest hunters of the prehistoric world. These dinosaurs had excellent eyesight, sharp teeth, and powerful claws. They were also very fast. They could run down other dinosaurs, like Iguanodon (ig-WAN-o-don), at speeds of up to forty miles per hour. And, like modern-day wolves, they may have hunted in packs.

Deinonychus

Allosaurus

Like other meat-eating dinosaurs, Allosaurus
(al-uh-SAWR-us) walked on two legs. Its long, heavy tail
stretched straight out behind it and helped Allosaurus
keep its balance.

For many years people thought that all dinosaurs were cold-blooded like reptiles. Cold-blooded dinosaurs would have had to warm their bodies in the sun before they could move around. But now some scientists believe that dinosaurs such as Allosaurus may have been warm-blooded like dogs and humans. They think that only a warm-blooded animal could have been as active as Allosaurus.

Camptosaurus
(KAMP-tuh-sawr-us)

Tyrannosaurus (tie-ran-oh-SAWR-us) was the largest meat-eating animal to ever walk the earth. It weighed more than a hippopotamus. Its body was as long as a line of five cars, and it was as tall as a two-story house.

Tyrannosaurus's head alone measured four feet,
and its mouth was equipped with six-inch teeth.
Its huge feet ended in eight-inch claws.

Tyrannosaurus

Hadrosaurus
(HAD-ruh-sawr-us)

Blue whale

Seismosaurus (size-mo-SAWR-us) may have been the
biggest dinosaur of them all. Its body could have been more
than one hundred feet in length—longer than a blue whale.
And this dinosaur may have weighed as much as ninety
tons. That's as heavy as fifteen elephants!

Seismosaurus

How did this plant-eating giant get enough food to keep it satisfied? Seismosaurus never stopped to chew. It may have swallowed small rocks along with the plants and leaves that it constantly scooped up. The stones ground up the plants and leaves in its stomach. That meant Seismosaurus could keep swallowing while its stomach was busy grinding the food already in it.

Pteranodon
(tare-AN-o-don)

While the dinosaurs ruled the land, other creatures took to the air. The most common of these were the flying reptiles called Pterosaurs (TAIR-uh-sawrs). Some were as small as sparrows. Others were huge, with wings that stretched out longer than a school bus.

Rhamphorhynchus
(ram-fo-RINK-us)

Pterosaurs were probably graceful in the air, but on land they waddled from place to place. Their wings may not have been strong enough for them to take off from the ground, so Pterosaurs may have had to launch themselves from cliffs.

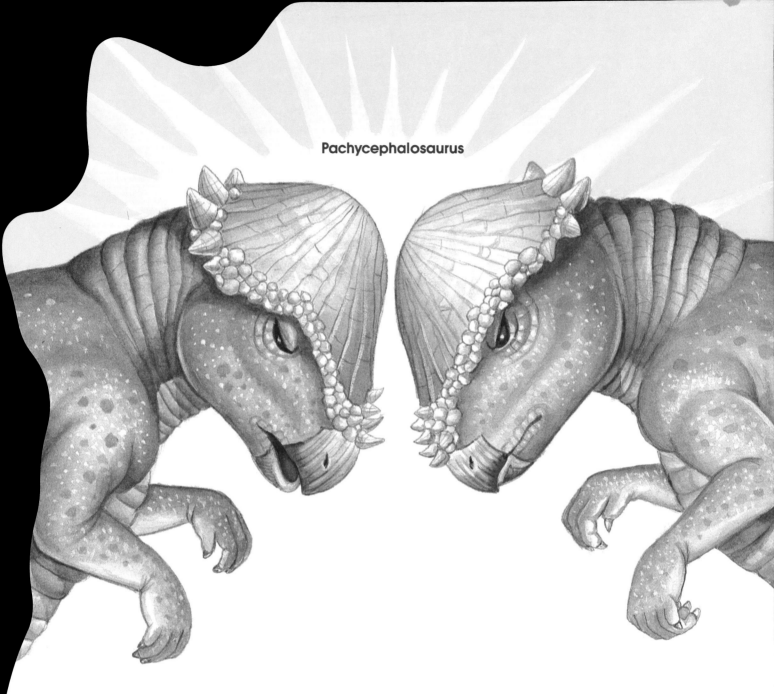

Pachycephalosaurus

The head of Pachycephalosaurus (pak-ee-SEF-uh-lo-SAWR-us) was covered with a layer of bone nine inches thick. It's possible that Pachycephalosaurus used its thick head for fighting. It could have fought off enemies by charging and head-butting. Males might have had ferocious head-banging contests to see who would attract the female.

Parasaurolophus (par-ah-SAWR-ol-uh-fus) had no sharp claws or horns to defend itself. Its protection was its keen hearing and sharp eyesight. The long hollow crest on its head might have helped it to smell better, too. Once it spotted an enemy, Parasaurolophus could escape by running, or even swimming, away.

Parasaurolophus

Triceratops

Triceratops (try-SAYR-ah-tops) and Ankylosaurus (ang-KILE-uh-sawr-us) lived 64 million years ago, when many fierce meat-eating dinosaurs roamed North America. Their bodies may have looked odd but helped keep them safe from hungry meat-eaters.

With its three sharp horns, Triceratops could do a lot of damage to an enemy. A Tyrannosaurus might have thought twice before attacking it.

Ankylosaurus looked like an armored tank. Its body was covered with sharp, bony plates. Even its eyelids were protected! If an enemy did approach, Ankylosaurus could break the enemy's legs by swinging its tail like a club.

Tyrannosaurus

Ankylosaurus

Triceratops and Ankylosaurus were two of the very last dinosaurs. About 64 million years ago something happened to cause these large dinosaurs to die out. What happened? One idea is that a huge asteroid crashed into Earth. The explosion from the asteroid's landing might have set off fires that burned huge areas of land. Perhaps dust and smoke blocked out sunlight and killed many plants and animals.

Each year scientists uncover new fossils to discover more about dinosaurs. Perhaps some day soon we will even know for certain why these amazing animals, who ruled Earth for 165 million years, vanished.